Away, Oh Wizard!

A CARD GAME FOR THE EARNEST APPRENTICE

Included with this book is a useful set of cards that may be used by apprentices to test their growing level of wizardological skill. The more games won, the greater the level of skill acquired, and the further the apprentice steps along the path of true wizardry.

HOW TO PLAY

- The envelope at the back of this book contains 24 wizard cards. There are six sets of four cards, each set representing a type of wizard and a selection of his associated items. The object of the game is to collect the highest number of complete sets. The game is best played by two players who should refresh their knowledge before starting by studying the cards that make up each set.
- Begin by shuffling the cards and tossing a coin to decide who deals first, then deal six cards to each player. The remaining cards go face down to form the draw pile.
- The dealer starts the game by asking his opponent for cards from a specific set. To do this the player must have at least two cards from that set already in his hand. He or she will also need to know which magical items go with each type of wizard, a true test of an apprentice's knowledge. For example, if a player has two grey cards (say the snake and the gryphon), he can ask for the Indian fakir and the apple of healing. Only one set of cards can be requested at a time. The other player must hand over any cards from that set that he has in his hand, provided that they are asked for by their correct name.
- A player's turn lasts until they are unsuccessful in getting the cards they ask for, or they make a mistake by requesting the wrong cards (for example, asking for the Indian fakir and the magic spyglass to complete the grey set). When either of these situations occur, their opponent should say "Away, Oh Wizard!" The player must then take a card from the draw pile and it is their opponent's turn to make a request.
- Once a player has collected a complete set, he should lay it face down on the table in front of him and continue his turn.
- If a player does not have two cards of the same colour or has no more cards left at his next turn, he should take a card from the draw pile and it becomes his opponent's turn. Once the draw pile has all gone, any player without cards is out of the game. When all six sets of cards have been made, the game is over. The player with the most sets is the winner. If both players have three sets, they must count up the scores for skill in animation, transformation, healing and affecting that appear in the corner of their wizard cards. Whoever has the highest total score is the Wizard Winner!

CONTENTS

Wizardology

A Guide to
Wizards of the World

Printed by C&C for
The Templar Company.
Edited for the modern Reader by
Dugald A. Steer and A. F. Wood
By Most Special Order. MDLXXVII.

QUID PRO QUO

MY FAITHFUL READER,

it has long been my *wish* to set down all I know about the *practices* of wizards throughout the known *world*.

 HE GREAT WORK IS, INDEED, GREAT, and it is my hope that by learning more about the wizarding ways of others, wizards the world over may add to their magical powers for the good of all.

I have written this book by magical means. It will only choose an owner who is worthy of learning the information I have set down within its pages so, if you are lucky enough to possess a copy, guard it well. It will tell you of the four wizardological paths: of Western wizards, Eastern sages, Chinese masters and shamans. Each one has its own unique skills in the various areas of magic.

All apprentices, even the most dull-witted, can learn much from the wisdom of others and, by playing the simple card game that I have thoughtfully included with this book, can measure the increase in their wizarding skills. The more games won, the greater the level of skill acquired. But rest not upon your laurels; no apprentice will succeed in becoming a true wizard by merely playing a game. Many years of diligent study, many more years of practice and decades of service to a truly great wizard such as myself will be needed before that is achieved!

AS I WILL, SO MOTE IT BE!

Merlin

Anno Domini 1577

WIZARDS OF THE WEST

Descendants of an ancient order, the wizards of the west must remember that power and responsibility go hand in hand.

HE WESTERN WIZARD is the custodian of a great body of magical knowledge, passed down through many centuries. Much of this wizarding skill originated with the ancient druids, but it has been added to over the years thanks to the Western wizard's love of travel. Much has been gleaned through communication with wizards from foreign lands, though wizards the world over would be wise to hone their own magical skills before starting to practise those perfected by others, and at all costs to avoid descent into the demonstration of magic for its own sake. Such exhibitionist tendencies almost always lead to trouble…

Where to find a WESTERN WIZARD :

Known throughout Western Europe; most villages and towns have their own resident wizard who will often be found demonstrating his powers in the town square, much to the delight of onlookers.

TABLE OF SKILLS

Animation	4	Particularly good at using animated objects to make light work of boring household tasks
Transformation	2	Most western wizards are nervous of transforming themselves; Puss-in-Boots is a popular cautionary tale
Healing	4	A keen interest in botany is recommended
Affecting	4	A skill best used in moderation
Divination	3	Obtaining a magical mirror is a short cut to success
Familiars		Cat, dog, toad, owl, hedgehog, pig; dragon, unicorn (rarely)

A wizard's outfit is all important. A selection of robes in assorted colours is advisable for they should be the correct hue for the type of spell to be performed (the appendix to this book will tell you all you need to know). They can be decorated with symbols to reinforce the magical identity of the wearer. A hat is a useful addition. It will keep a wizard's ears warm and can be a handy hiding place for small items. Pointed hats, however, are a wholly unnecessary affectation.

GOOD SPIRITS

All wizards need the help of good spirits to make their magic work. Familiars can help with this, for they can see and communicate easily with creatures who so often choose to keep themselves hidden from human sight. However, even the cleverest familiar may occasionally fall foul of a wicked imp or sprite, as can be seen from the illustration below. Imps are a tricksy lot and best left to their own devices.

FAMILIARS

Every wizard will benefit from having a pet animal, known as a familiar. They are the wizard's true friend and, whether an ordinary animal or a magical one, can teach him a great deal. Typical familiars associated with Western wizards include cats, dogs, owls, toads, hedgehogs and, on rare occasions, helpful pigs.

WESTERN WIZARD

WIZARD EQUIPMENT

Wizards the world over recognise the value of a good and well-kept collection of magical equipment. The accomplished wizard can use magic to transform everyday objects into magical ones for permanent use—an ordinary stick into a wand, for example, or a broom into a handy transportation device. Other magical items might be passed down from wizard to apprentice, gaining power commensurate with their age.

Magical Items for Western Wizards :

The collection below shows seven items that all Western wizards should strive to obtain. Some are easier to come by than others. It may take a wizard many years to locate a pair of magical boots, whilst cauldrons can be made to measure by most local blacksmiths.

1. Spell Book—Only a few have magical properties; mainly useful as a place to store information.
2. Magical Mirror—A useful means of divination. Some mirrors, however, cannot always be relied upon to tell the truth.
3. Seven League Boots—Useful for long journeys, these books can cover great distances in one step.
4. Cauldron—Useful for the making of potions as well as lunch.
5. Wand—An essential item for all.
6. Athame—A wizard's knife used for the making of wands.

Sigillum Mysteriorum :

The Sigillum is a powerful tool for the making and reading of codes written in symbols. All Western wizards are well practised in this art, and seldom write their spells any other way. Some extremely clever wizards make it their business to collect rare and complicated codes to tax the brains of the less bright.

Magical Transportation :

Although Western wizards have the power to animate commonplace items in order to transport themselves from one place to another, many eschew the delights of flying broomsticks, chairs or even beds, preferring to rely on the most straightforward means available—the use of their own legs.

Fig. 1: Spell Book

Fig. 2: Magical Mirror

Fig. 4: Cauldron

Fig. 5: Wand

Fig. 6: Athame

Fig. 3: Seven League Boots

TAMING DRAGONS

Another class of familiar available to the accomplished wizard is that of the magical animal. Western wizards are often adept at befriending dragons, but care must be taken at all times for they can be temperamental creatures and fatalities among the inexperienced are not uncommon. When trying to tame a dragon, a good stock of riddles is useful. However, dragonology is a tricky field of study that cannot be fully covered here and the diligent apprentice should seek out a more complete treatment of the subject.

DRAGON SPELL

Hold a magically-charged talisman aloft and repeat the following verse eight times. At the ninth reading, a dragon will appear.

Nine times nine lives hath lived the cat
And ninety nights are nine by ten.
Nine ounces from nine pounds of fat;
Nine times hath pecked the Dorking hen,
So nine times nine I'll call to thee;
Nine of those nine, come thou to me!

MAGICAL CREATURES

Great respect is due to the veritable *menagerie* of *magical creatures*
that may make themselves available to help good *wizards* in their work.

 HE HELP OF A MAGICAL CREATURE can add greatly to a wizard's power, but only if that help is given willingly. Any attempt to force a creature, magical or otherwise, to help you against its will is destined to end in trouble.

This is seldom a problem for most wizards, for whom a love and respect for the natural world is second nature, but novices to the art must be encouraged to learn as much as they can about the rarer magical beasts, their appearance and uses, the better to be prepared for any unexpected encounter.

Fairies :

Circles in the woods made from rings of toadstools are a good place to summon fairies and other helpful spirits. These invisible creatures may reveal themselves to you if you practise the Summoning Spell opposite, and are essential for the correct working of many spells. Should they appear, beware of believing everything they say. They are adept at making fools of all but the wisest of wizards.

Wyverns :

A species of dragon from the African continent. The shed scales from a wyvern's wing, ground to a powder and mixed with water, can help the user see over incredible distances.

SUMMONING SPELL

Walk clockwise around the inside of a fairy ring, casting salt mixed with a little dragon dust as you go, and whisper:

Fairy beings I can't see,
Please will you appear to me?
Help me, help me if you would;
My spell is only meant for good.
VENIO, ADVOCO, VIDEO!

A word of warning: Never attempt to summon the help of spirits to practise dark magic. Misfortune awaits any wizard who chooses such a path.

Unicorns :

Unicorns usually make themselves known only to female wizards and are most often found in places where they can find adequate peace and quiet. Though they have a loud bray, they hate noise.

Phoenix :

Though extremely rare, the feather of a phoenix can be used to enhance the strength of many spells. They are particularly effective when used for anything concerned with magical transportation.

Gryphons :

Temperamental creatures, gryphons have a natural instinct for finding treasure, particularly gold.

Mermaids :

Mermaids can be useful allies to any wizard contemplating a sea voyage. They have the power to calm even the roughest of waves; if stormy weather seems likely, enlist the help of a mermaid to ensure safe passage.

SHAMANS

Theirs is a *difficult* path, but it is also the one that takes the user closest to the *natural world* and its many *wonders*.

 HAMANS ARE TO BE FOUND ON ALL THE CONTINENTS of the known world, from the so-called "witch doctors" of Africa to the powerful tribal warriors of North and South America. They are masters of spell-casting, often using the most simple of materials, and have perhaps the greatest understanding of, and power over, the natural world. This comes in part from the deep reverence they show to all creatures and which, in turn, enables them to excel at the art of transformation into animal form, often from a very early age.

SHAMANS OF THE WORLD

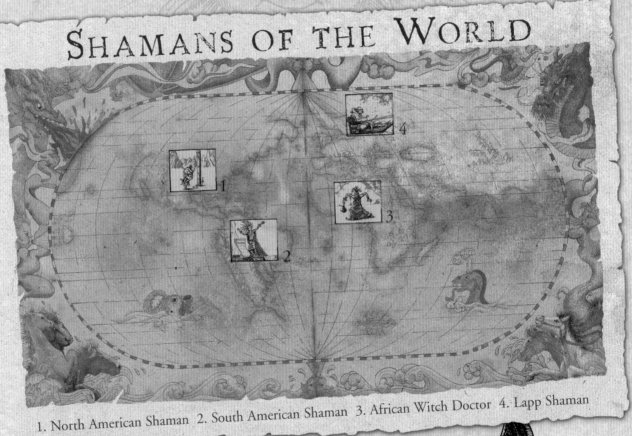

1. North American Shaman 2. South American Shaman 3. African Witch Doctor 4. Lapp Shaman

◦⊶ SHAPE-SHIFTERS ⊷◦

Masters of transformation, shamans can shape-shift into many animal forms, enabling them to fly like an eagle, fight like a bear or swim like a killer whale at will. However, this useful skill cannot be acquired without first gaining a full understanding of the creature involved. Since this is best achieved through close personal observation, it is not an undertaking to be embarked upon lightly, especially where bears or killer whales are concerned.

FAMILIARS

Shamans rarely call on the help of magical creatures, preferring to use spells to transfer magical properties to the ordinary beasts of our Earth. Any creature showing strange behavioural traits may prove to be under the effects of a shaman's spell or, indeed, be the shaman himself in animal form.

STARGAZING

Centaurus	Scorpio	Gemini

All shamans are experts at starcraft. Rather than using the night-time heavens for magical purposes, they tend to refer to them as one would a map, to help them keep their sense of direction on the ground.

SHAMAN

AMPHITHERES

One of the most useful magical creatures available to the South American shaman is the winged serpent or amphithere. A type of dragon, their feathers can be used in healing potions and, when used to stir a drink made of certain forest fruits, will give the imbiber the strength of ten men.

SOUTH AMERICAN SHAMANS

None have been so *feared* in their time as the great
and *powerful* wizards of Central and South America.

WITH THEIR FEATHERED headdresses and colourful robes, the wizards of Central and South America can be a fearful sight. Not fearful enough, however, to protect their people from the Conquistadors who even now are pillaging their temples in search of treasure. These temples, wonders of construction often hidden deep in the jungles found in this part of the world, were often built by magical means. The jungles, also called forests of rain, are also a great source of creatures that, with a little patience, can make useful familiars. Snakes can contribute greatly to a fearsome appearance whilst parrots, although extremely intelligent and capable of learning a great many spells, can also be noisy to the point of irritation.

TABLE OF SKILLS

Animation	3	Usually employed to assist with the building of temples or other impressive structures
Transformation	4	Sometimes recreate the form of the great Aztec winged serpent Quetzalcoatl with fearsome results
Healing	4	
Affecting	3	Known for affecting Conquistadors with a terrible—if temporary—curse known as 'Montezuma's Revenge'
Divination	2	
Familiars		Snake, parrot, quetzal, guinea pig (in mountain regions); amphithere

NORTH AMERICAN SHAMANS

The greatest of *healers*, the vast open spaces of the *New World* are home to these master *herbalists* of the *wizarding* world.

HE SHAMANS OF NORTH AMERICA have a deep understanding of the natural world. They can talk to almost all species of animal and know the uses of most types of plant, preparing healing potions and poultices from ancient recipes. Instead of recording their knowledge in books, it is passed down verbally. Similarly, these powerful workers of true magic tend to shun the elaborate trappings of modern life, choosing simple stones, bones, sticks or feathers as their magical items, endowing them with enormous power through use of their ancient spellcraft. They are also masters of the art of dream-catching and can control the dreams of others. If you suddenly start dreaming of herds of buffalo you may have been unknowingly in contact with a shaman.

Round and round the totem pole :
Many shamans focus magical force by dancing and chanting round a pole, known as a totem.

∞ TABLE OF SKILLS ∞

Animation	2	
Transformation	5	*Adept at taking the form of many types of animal; groups of shaman sometimes form herds*
Healing	5	*Poultices and potions galore*
Affecting	5	*Rarely used for anything other than talking to animals*
Divination	2	
Familiars		*Eagle, crow, owl, hawk or other bird, occasionally baby buffalo or bear cub*

Feathered Friends :
Shamans often choose birds as their familiars. Eagles, crows, owls and hawks are all popular choices; the newly-introduced chicken is also gaining favour, as its eggs are useful for breakfast.

FLYING SPELL

Cast into a fire three pinches of dried tumbleweed, four cloudberries and the tail feather of an eagle who has flown thrice round the sun and chant:

Fly me to the moon.
Fly me to the sun.
Fly me to the stars.
My flying spell's begun.

You will be able to fly like an eagle until darkness falls.

NORTH AMERICAN

LAPP SHAMANS

From the four corners of the *globe*, each community of *shamans* uses their own system of *wizardology* to work their magic.

HE POWER OF THE CHANT is central to shamanic magic. Different chants may be used to bestow magical power onto items made of bone, leather or horn, or to help focus the mind to produce magical effects. Chanting can be done by the shaman alone or sometimes in a group, often sitting in a circle around a fire or an item of ancient magical significance—a tree or arrangement of stones. The chief shaman, often known as the "elder", will lead the chant, often speaking in his own language but sometimes using animal sounds or words that imitate or conjure the sound of nature itself. This is particularly so when creating a chant designed to control the weather.

Wise Men:
Shamans have no need of money and riches. They most often work for the benefit of those who live locally to them, and are protectors of the land in which they live. Their payment is often no more than the gratitude of those whom they have helped.

Weather Spells :

All shamans are experienced in creating magical items that have influence over the forces of nature. A wind knot, made by chanting whilst tying knots in a simple length of leather, can summon or calm a gale. Other weather chants are associated with certain animals. The "song of the whale" can effect a storm at sea, the "chant of the snow bear" can conjure a snowstorm, whilst the "song of the snowy owl" can cause the snows to melt.

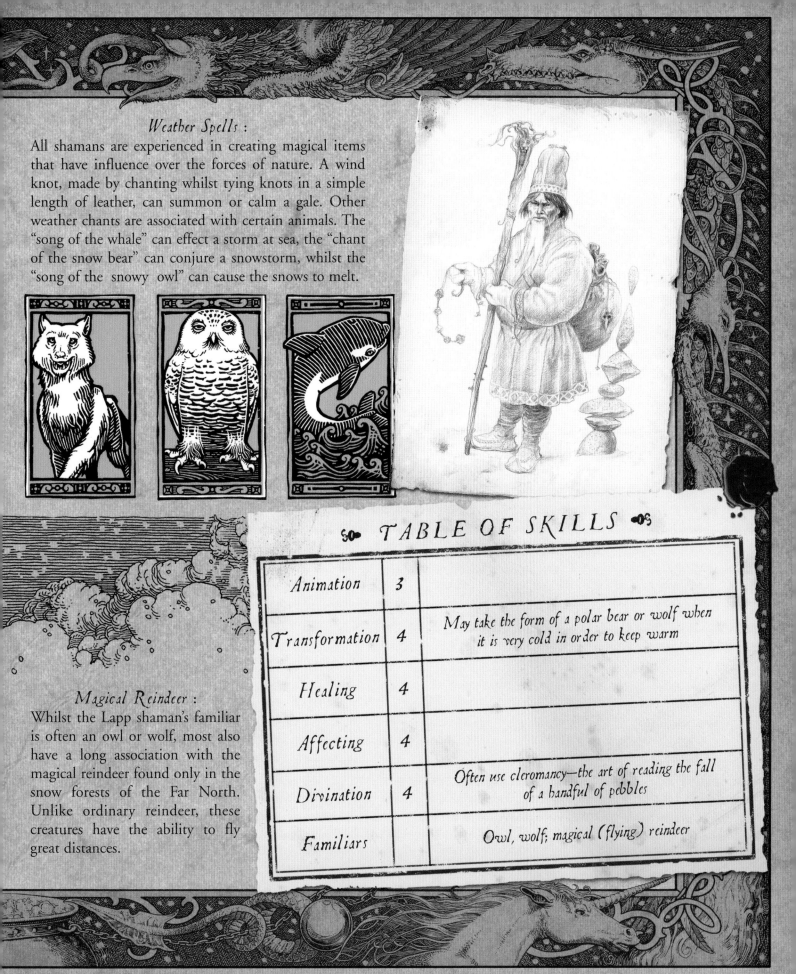

Magical Reindeer :

Whilst the Lapp shaman's familiar is often an owl or wolf, most also have a long association with the magical reindeer found only in the snow forests of the Far North. Unlike ordinary reindeer, these creatures have the ability to fly great distances.

TABLE OF SKILLS

Animation	3	
Transformation	4	May take the form of a polar bear or wolf when it is very cold in order to keep warm
Healing	4	
Affecting	4	
Divination	4	Often use cleromancy—the art of reading the fall of a handful of pebbles
Familiars		Owl, wolf; magical (flying) reindeer

AFRICAN SHAMANS

Medicine *men* or *witch doctors*?
The *shamans* of Africa are often misunderstood.

HE WIZARDS OF CENTRAL AFRICA have a great love of elaborate costumes, often donning masks, headdresses and other paraphernalia to perform their spells, and accompanying the reading of the spell itself with all manner of dancing and mumbo-jumbo. This is entirely unnecessary but, along with their unfounded reputation for commanding evil spirits, has led them to be greatly feared, especially by strangers. This often works to the wizard's advantage since he tends to be left alone to hone his powerful healing skills instead of being constantly pestered by those seeking magical cures for the most minor of ailments.

Like their costumes, African shamans often choose a familiar designed to impress. Lions, leopards or cheetahs are popular choices, although elephants, rhinoceroses and even hippopotamuses have been known. The latter are not to be recommended to any but the most experienced since they have a reputation for being uncontrollable, coupled with having a very nasty bite.

TABLE OF SKILLS

Animation	2	
Transformation	3	
Healing	5	Their reputation for being able to heal all illness has led to their alternative name of "medicine men"
Affecting	5	Can affect the behaviour of others with ease
Divination	1	
Familiars		Lion, leopard, cheetah, occasionally one of the larger African mammals such as the elephant; wyvern (rarely)

INDIAN FAKIRS

Among the *wisest* of all wizards, *fakirs* avoid all *involvement* in worldly affairs.

OF ALL THE WIZARDS OF THE WORLD, the fakirs of India are amongst the most mysterious. Little is known of their magic since they rarely speak, often choosing to remove themselves from the everyday world and instead spend months in curious pursuits such as balancing on one leg, or laying on a bed of nails. This helps them to focus their minds and concentrate their wizardly powers so that whenever they do speak it is to utter only words of the purest wisdom.

℘ TABLE OF SKILLS ℘

Animation	1	
Transformation	2	
Healing	4	
Affecting	2	
Divination	5	Their tremendous wisdom also helps in this area— if you can get them to talk
Familiars		Snake, particularly cobra

℘ GREAT SNAKES ℘

The fakir often shuns all human possessions, owning nothing, and wearing only rags. However, as with all wizards, fakirs recognise the value of having a familiar and often choose a snake, particularly a cobra. They are also masters of the art of ophiomancy—a form of divination involving the reading of signs obtained by observing a pit of writhing snakes.

ARABIAN SAGES

The pursuit and *love* of *knowledge* marks the true path of the *Arabian* sage.

VERY SAGE KNOWS THE VALUE OF A GOOD BOOK. Books are the means by which they pass down the wisdom of the ancients and many spend their lives searching for rare titles to add to their libraries. They are masters of spells concerned with animation, and passionate collectors (and creators) of beautiful and unusual magical objects. Often amassing a great treasure trove of valuables, the sages' weakness for riches and the finer things in life can sometimes be their downfall, turning them away from the practice of magic for the benefit of others to spells and enchantments designed only to feed their own greed. Needless to say, such behaviour almost always ends in disaster, most often due to the sage falling foul of a nefarious genie or other magical spirit who will trick them into parting with their treasures only to leave them with nothing.

❧ TABLE OF SKILLS ❧

Animation	5	*Particularly adept at animations involving flight, especially if they have a friendship with a phoenix*
Transformation	3	*Rarely interested in transforming themselves but often use spells to enhance the richness of their robes*
Healing	2	
Affecting	4	
Divination	2	*Performance in this area can be improved by ownership of a magical spyglass*
Familiars		*Monkey, scorpion, horse, phoenix*

FIRST CLASS FLIGHT

Whilst typically choosing to animate carpets or rugs, some wizards choose more robust items as their flying devices. Old wooden trunks can be particularly valuable in this regard, especially for long journeys or when transporting items of value from one place to another.

Where to find an ARABIAN SAGE

Sages are found throughout Arabia, Persia and North Africa. It is thought that much of their knowledge originated with the great wizards of Ancient Egypt.

Genies:

All sages are expert in dealing with genies, also known as djinn or jinnis, but even the greatest sage knows that they should be accorded the greatest respect. Western wizards who might be unlucky enough to release a genie (for they are often trapped in lamps, bottles or jars) would be wise to beware the offer of three wishes, often proffered by genies who find themselves released. These ancient spirits are notorious tricksters and the safest response by far is to simply grant them their freedom, although it is permissible to use two of the wishes for the good of others.

⊷ TO SCRY OR NOT TO SCRY ⊷

The sages of Arabia, Persia and North Africa are also adept at scrying, a form of divination that involves gazing at a smooth surface in order to see into the future or ascertain the answer to certain questions. It will come as no surprise that their favourite scrying item is a gemstone, preferably a star sapphire or ruby. Alternatively, a magical telescope or spyglass—the Spyglass of Revealing—is a popular collector's item.

THREE RULES

When flying a carpet,
remember the following:

* Always keep your eyes on
the sky ahead in order to
avoid collision with tall
buildings or trees.
* If you are an inexperienced
flier, wear a safety harness or,
preferably, a parachute.
* Never fly too fast—a safe
flight is a slow flight.

EASTERN MASTERS

Meditation and *contemplation* are essential for the development of *wisdom* and *intuition* in the Eastern masters.

ASTERN MASTERS, MORE THAN ANY OTHER WIZARDS, are concerned with the inner workings of the human mind. They spend a great deal of time just thinking and are unconcerned with the possession of worldly goods or the ability to perform showy magic. The simplicity of their appearance, indeed their lives, should not cause their power to be underestimated, for they are masters of the art of divination. There is no wizard better qualified to give advice to others than the Eastern master.

Stamp Magic :

Eastern masters are experts at the practice of stamp magic, where symbols stamped into clay or earth can be given magical power to protect the bearer. The Dragon Tiger Stamp opposite provides protection from attack by tigers. Other forms of stamp magic can allow the master to walk through fire without being burned, to be impervious to the cold, or to perform acts of superhuman strength.

Tortoise Time :

The familiar of choice for an Eastern master is the humble tortoise. Like their masters, they live to a great age, have enormous wisdom and like to take all things slowly.

◦ TABLE OF SKILLS ◦

Animation	2	
Transformation	2	The most accomplished masters can transform themselves into the four basic elements—Air, Earth, Fire or Water
Healing	4	Most believe the power of the mind can heal all ills
Affecting	2	
Divination	5	Look no further for wise advice than the words of the master
Familiars		Tortoise, panda (rarely); lung dragon

Most Eastern masters
live in the more remote
mountain regions of Indo-
China, often dwelling
in temples, monasteries
or, occasionally, caves.

EASTERN MASTER

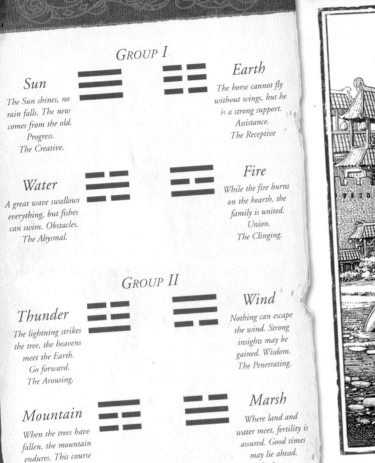

Group I

Sun
The Sun shines, no rain falls. The new comes from the old. Progress. The Creative.

Earth
The horse cannot fly without wings, but he is a strong support. Assistance. The Receptive

Water
A great wave swallows everything, but fishes can swim. Obstacles. The Abysmal.

Fire
While the fire burns on the hearth, the family is united. Union. The Clinging.

Group II

Thunder
The lightning strikes the tree, the heavens meet the Earth. Go forward. The Arousing.

Wind
Nothing can escape the wind. Strong insights may be gained. Wisdom. The Penetrating.

Mountain
When the trees have fallen, the mountain endures. This course seems right. Keeping Still.

Marsh
Where land and water meet, fertility is assured. Good times may lie ahead. The Joyous.

∞ THE I CHING ∞

A popular method of divination, the I Ching is based on the reading of eight trigrams, the meanings of which are detailed above. As with all forms of divination, the answer must be revealed by chance and be interpreted by the wisdom of the diviner. To use this simplified version of the I Ching, toss a coin. If it shows heads, use the trigrams from Group I above; if tails, use Group II. Toss the coin again. If heads, choose the top row; if tails, choose the bottom. Now toss the coin a third time. If heads, choose the trigram on the left; if tails, use the trigram on the right.
All is now revealed.

∞ DIVINATION ∞

The eastern master uses many methods to divine the future. The formation of scattered yarrow sticks or the pattern of a handful of thrown pebbles, the swirl of water over rocks or the flicker of a candle flame can all be "read", but only by the most experienced practitioners of the art. Apprentices should not rely on their divinatory powers, and certainly not offer them as a service to others, until they have proved themselves through many years of correct predictions.

ಐ LUNG DRAGONS ⊘

Eastern masters are often the protectors of the magical lung dragons found throughout the mountains of Indo-China. The association between wizards and dragons dates back many thousands of years, to 2962 B.C. when Fu Hsi, a powerful Chinese master, was taught the great skill and art of writing by a dragon and a magical bond was formed that has lasted until today.

龍鳳
虎馬

LUNG DRAGON

AN APPRENTICE'S APPENDIX

The following pages include essential information for any apprentice to the great art of wizardology. Learn it well, for without it no true progress in magic will be possible.

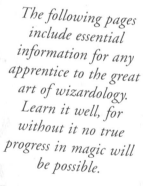

THE PATH OF LEARNING

can be full of pitfalls. Never be tempted to stray into practising the dark arts or any spells that could be considered negative. Work only for the good of others and all will, hopefully, be well.

SPELLCRAFT

The wise apprentice will let practice and secrecy be his watchwords. Practice will make your spellcraft perfect, but may take a lifetime. Secrecy is of the utmost importance—once you have mastered the workings of a spell, keep it to yourself. Magic that is bandied about can lose its power or be turned against you.

THE FOUR MAIN CLASSES OF SPELL

Animating Spells :

Animating spells cause objects or creatures to move in a desired fashion. They are some of the easiest spells to master. In the West, they make use of the Fire spirit, Pranxtor.

Transforming Spells :

Transforming spells make one thing appear to be another. Equally, they can cause things to disappear altogether. Though some such spells can be fixed so that the transformation lasts, sometimes for hundreds of years, most can be undone very simply by, for example, a kiss. In the Western system of magic, they are associated with the Water spirit, Gladde.

Healing Spells :

Only the most powerful wizards should attempt healing spells as they require a great deal of energy if they are to work properly. Never try to heal another or yourself unless you have at least one hundred years' experience in the healing arts and much practice in contacting the spirits Jaypes and Larfor who support such good works. Go to the doctor instead.

Affecting Spells :

These spells are forbidden as a rule for they can change they way that people think or feel. They can also be used to enable the wizard to communicate with spirits, magical creatures and animals. As with animating spells, they make use of Pranxtor and are more likely to go wrong than any other type of magic.

THE FOUR SEASONAL SPIRITS

Much of the magic of Western wizards is based on the use of four magical elements, each of which is linked to both a season and one of four playful spirits. Though many alternative magical helpmates—from fairies and imps to genies, dryads and myriad others—can be called upon, the inexperienced apprentice should make good use of these four until he becomes more accomplished. They can be summoned by reciting the spells below whilst imagining their symbol glowing:

GLADDE
Spirit of Water and Spring; helps with creative magic.

GATKA ATGA, BUDS IN MAY. SPRING IS SPRUNG, IT'S TIME TO PLAY.

PRANXTOR
Spirit of Fire and Summer; useful in works of strength.

HOT AND DRY, SUMMERS FLY. DRY AND HOT, PRANXTOR'S GOT.

JAYPES
Spirit of Air and Autumn; helps bring wisdom.

LAUGH AND JOKE WITH JAYPES FOR NO FOOL ESCAPES; LEAVES WILL FALL FROM SKIES, HIS WORD IS: WIDDERSHINSWISE.

LARFOR
Spirit of Earth and Winter; useful with assisting change.

THE COLD WIND BLOWS UP LARFOR'S NOSE, SO RED IT GLOWS. WHO WOULD SUPPOSE IT FREEZES TOES?

ALL SELF-RESPECTING WESTERN WIZARDS need a laboratory or workshop in which to store their collection of magical equipment and books, and in which to practise their spell-casting skills. If you do not have a whole room at your disposal, a corner of one will do. Ensure you collect the following as a priority:

* Set of robes
* Spell Book (keep hidden at all times)
* Familiar (Do not attempt to use anything too elaborate; your pet mouse will do to start with.)
* Wand
* Books (A library of a hundred well-thumbed tomes is the minimum requirement; learn all you can about everything. A dictionary, an encyclopaedia and an atlas are essential.)
* Star Map
* Potions, ointments and ingredients for spells
* Amulets, talismans and other magical items
* Crystal Ball
* Magic Mirror
* Cauldron

Spell Book

SYMBOLS AND THEIR MEANINGS
Use these symbols, shown on the right, to adorn your robes and wands and decorate your Spell Books.

SPELL-CASTING TABLE

Use the following table of correspondences to formulate simple spells. Remember, with magic,
a length of wood may become a powerful wand and an ordinary object, a magical one.

Planet		Spell	Day	Colour	Beast	Wood	Element	Seal
Moon	☽	Transforming	Monday	Silver	Dolphin	Willow	Water : Gladde	
Mercury	☿	Healing	Tuesday	Yellow	Owl	Hazel	Air : Jaypes	
Venus	♀	Affecting	Friday	Green	Dove	Olive	Fire : Pranxtor	
Sun	☉	Animating	Sunday	Orange	Lion	Oak	Fire : Pranxtor	
Mars	♂	Combating	Thursday	Red	Hawk	Birch	Fire : Pranxtor	
Jupiter	♃	Bringing Justice	Wednesday	Blue	Wolf	Cherry	Air : Jaypes	
Saturn	♄	Altering Time	Saturday	Violet	Dragon	Yew	Earth : Larfor	

PLANETARY SYMBOLS

☽ *Moon* ☿ *Mercury* ♀ *Venus* ☉ *Sun*
♂ *Mars* ♃ *Jupiter* ♄ *Saturn*

ELEMENTAL SYMBOLS

△ *Air* ▽ *Earth* △ *Fire* ▽ *Water*

ALCHEMICAL SYMBOLS

⚨ *Iron* ♇ *Tin* ⊧ *Poisonous* ☿ *Mercury*
♆ *Antimony* ♄ *Lead* ♀ *Copper* ♇ *Vitriol*

THE UNIVERSAL SIGILLUM

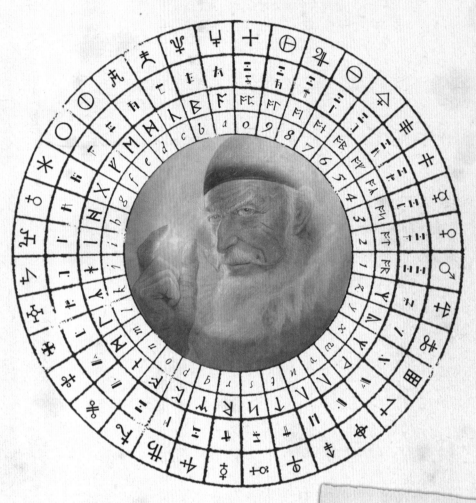

All wizards should be accomplished in the use of codes. You can make up your own by choosing new symbols to correspond with the 26 letters of the Western alphabet and the numbers 1 to 9. In the meantime, use one of the four codes above to write secret messages to other wizardologists.

Key to the
SIGILLUM

Outer ring: Common wizard code
Second ring: Lambert script
Third ring: Dragon runes
Inner ring: English

A WORD
OF
WARNING

THOSE WHO STUDY the art of wizardology must remember the cardinal rule that all magic should be used only for good ends. Helpful, positive thoughts aimed at assisting others may bring helpful, positive results. Unhelpful, negative thoughts are more likely to rebound on the sender, for all wizards the world over are subject to a powerful magical law known as the Rule of Three. This rule states that negative magic will rebound on the sender with three times more force than that with which it was sent out.

Never bother the spirits for trifles, or merely to benefit yourself, for even the greatest wizards have occasionally come unstuck by straying from the true wizardological path. Keep this in mind at all times and one day you too may become a Wizard of the World.

AS I WILL, SO MOTE IT BE!

Merlin

Anno Domini 1577

First published in the *UK* in 2007 by TEMPLAR PUBLISHING,
an imprint of *The Templar Company Plc*,
Pippbrook Mill, London Road, Dorking, Surrey, RH4 1JE, UK

✠

Illustration Copyright © 2006 John Howe,
Anne Yvonne Gilbert, Tomislav Tomic and Helen Ward.
Text and Design Copyright © 2006 *The Templar Company Plc*.
Wizardology™ is a trademark of The Templar Company Plc.
Designed by *Jonathan Lambert* and *Nghiem Ta*.
Anglo-Saxon Runes font by *Daniel Steven Smith*.

✠

Publisher's Note: Over the *Centuries* a *Number*
of *Books* have laid *Claim* to having been penned by
a certain *Wizard* named *Master Merlin*, but
few have dared to provide true *Instruction*
for wizardological *Apprentices*.
The *Publisher* does not recommend
meddling in magical *Matters*,
and cautions those who
do so only to attempt
Spells for the *Good*
of *Others*.

✠

templar publishing

✠ www.wizardology.com ✠